Andrew was a contributor to a weekly radio programme on the arts for more than three years. He has been an advisor to a number of theatres in London including Shakespeare's Globe and Mountview Academy of Theatrical Arts. Andrew also appeared in the millennium edition of *Blackadder*.

He is a board member for the Red Rose Chain Film, and Theatre Company.

His latest publication was a collection of comedy sketches entitled *A Nipperkin of Bunkum*.

Dedication

Many special thanks to my wife Muriel for her ideas, contributions and help with proofreading this book.
Also to my sons Alex and Richard and friend Jean Baker for their suggestions.

Andrew Ings

FROM PAGE TO STAGE

ISBN 978 14963 549 3

www.austinmacauley.com

First Published (2014)
Austin Macauley Publishers Ltd.
25 Canada Square
Canary Wharf
London
E14 5LB

Printed and Bound in Great Britain

A Nipperkin Of Bunkum

Also by Andrew Ings

The series of short scripts are set in a variety of different situations.

In one play a talk-show host meets his antithesis in the guise of art critic Hughe Perciman-Smythe, and in another an eighty five year old man is planning his stag night with his friends.

Throughout, satire can be found regarding the art world, Health and Safety regulations gone mad, the annoyance of calling directory enquiries, a cross-dressing initiative at a rather forward-thinking office and many others.

In these days of political correctness are you sick of not being able to say what you would really like to?

Andrew has written a collection of comedy sketches and monologues for performance that speak for many of us.

Andrew has extensive experience in theatre including acting, directing and reviewing. Based on some of his own experiences of life, these sketches are topical and some might argue slightly outrageous, saying what many of us are thinking but in a very funny way. They are very simple to stage and have casts of just two or three.

If you believe in giving your audience a good laugh, you will certainly enjoy staging these sketches and monologues.

Contents

Scriptum – A Poem

I am a play
That demands to be heard
My body – the action
My blood – the word

I am a play
Created by toil
Not for directors or
Actors to spoil

My story in telling
May excite or impress
It depends on the actors
And where they put stress

So study me well
And study me sound
Then in the telling
My story'll be round

So directors and actors
Please treat me with zeal
Rehearse me and nurse me
Till my soul you reveal

Then for the public
At last I am born
With make-up and lights
And flats on the boards

Now I'm over and done
Till next time around
The lights are all dimmed
The sound is all gone

When next you consider
That acting's the thing
Just remember, don't dither
Role playing's the king

Preface

Five minutes to go and the dressing room is a hive of activity. Amid the hubbub of the final moments before the tabs open, an anxious face peers at the reflected mask like some long-ago Narcissus.

The director rushes in, "I suggest a touch more grey at the temple," and rushes out again.

Around you the usual trivial conversation:

"I nearly didn't get here tonight" or "by the way what is this play called?"

The two-minute bell sounds and the pulse quickens.

Enter stage manager, "Beginners please. John please remember the pistol is in the right-hand drawer".

A glance in the mirror and a smudge of powder covers a shiny nose. More comings and goings, well-wishers, usually other club members. In pops the house manager, exclaiming "full house tonight, don't cut it."

The house lights dim, the audience hushes and the nerves begin to bite--thirty seconds and I'm on, damn I need to go to the loo.

This is a scene familiar to anyone who is or has been involved in Amateur Theatre. After weeks of rehearsals, stage construction, the making of props, costumes, painting, publicity and a hundred and one other things, your first night arrives.

While desperately trying to remember your opening line, you promise yourself a backstage job next time…if there is a next time.

There will be of course, because drama is addictive, there is no doubt about that. It's a drug and once you are hooked you can't shake it off.

But then to be any sort of addict you have to be slightly mad.

Introduction

This guide is intended to help those who wish to embark on the road to staging an amateur theatrical production.

Amateur Theatre has been a part of our national life for generations, its significance being recognised by Geoffrey Whitworth in 1919 when he founded the British Drama League. There are now groups in many parts of the country.

It has been a part of my life for approaching fifty years and has given me an interesting, demanding, sometimes compromising, often amusing, and always rewarding leisure activity.

Through Amateur Theatre I have become involved in the professional theatre, reviewed many productions for radio and newspapers and writing has developed into a major part of my life.

Over the years many groups have been the butt of music-hall jokes, sometimes deserved, sometimes not. The best groups are as good as the local repertory companies, and the worst? Well, the less said the better.

Why we tie ourselves up a few nights a week for several weeks, building sets, learning lines and all the rest is something of a mystery to those not involved.

To those who are however, it is a classless, ageless hobby which is very rewarding.

It could also be said in these days of stress at work to be a thoroughly relaxing activity.

The mention of Amateur Dramatics to anybody who has never experienced a production often brings exclamations of derision.

Images are immediately conjured up of collapsing scenery, actors and actresses peering at the audience looking for family or friends, and of the prompt going home at the first interval with a sore throat.

On the other hand those involved realise the tremendous efforts that go into any production.

Belonging to a local theatre group can be mentally stimulating and great fun, as well as giving one a feeling of doing something for the community.

When prospective new members are approached they sometimes quake in their shoes at the thought of going on stage.

The fact is there are very often more people "in the wings" than "on the boards" during a production.

Amateur Theatre is very much a team effort with the objective being the best possible production. It is tremendous fun, but not a free ride. It requires commitment of time and energy, with the smallest job equal in importance to the greatest part.

Background, education, job and class are all irrelevant. It is after all a social group with a common aim and well worthwhile.

Tongue-In-Cheek Definitions

Eternity
The time that passes between a dropped cue and the next line.

Prop
An object small enough to be lost by an actor 30 seconds before it is needed on stage.

Director
The individual who suffers from the delusion that they are responsible for every moment of brilliance mentioned in the local paper.

Blocking
The art of moving actors on the stage in such a manner as not to collide with the walls, the furniture, the orchestra pit or each other.

Blocking Rehearsal
A rehearsal taking place early in the production schedule, where actors frantically write down movements which will be nowhere in evidence by opening night.

Quality Theatre
Any show with which you were directly involved.

Turkey
Every show with which you were not directly involved.

Dress Rehearsal
Rehearsal that becomes a whole new ball game as actors attempt to manoeuvre among the 49 objects that the set designer added at 7:30 that evening.

Tech week
The last week of rehearsal when everything that was supposed to be done weeks before finally comes together at the last minute. Reaches its grand climax on dress rehearsal night when costumes rip, a dimmer pack catches fire and the director has a nervous breakdown. Also known as *hell week*.

Set
An obstacle course which, throughout the rehearsal period, defies the laws of physics by growing smaller week by week while continuing to occupy the same amount of space.

Monologue
That shining moment when all eyes are focused on a single actor who is desperately aware that if he forgets a line, no one can save him.

Dark Night
The night before opening when no rehearsal is scheduled so the actors and crew can go home and get some well-deserved rest, but instead spend the night staring sleeplessly at the ceiling because they're sure they needed one more rehearsal.

Bit Part
An opportunity for the actor with the smallest role to count everybody else's lines and mention repeatedly that he or she has the smallest part in the show.

Green Room
Room shared by nervous actors waiting to go on stage and the precocious children whose actor parents couldn't get a babysitter that night.

Dark Spot
An area of the stage which the lighting designer has inexplicably forgotten to light, and which has a magnetic attraction for the first-time actor.

Serious Definitions

Stage left/right
Sides of the stage when looking at the audience

Down stage
Moving towards the audience

Up stage
Moving towards the rear of the stage

Wings
The space each side of the stage out of view of the audience

Fly Space
Space above the stage

Props
Items that are used by the cast during performance

Pros
Proscenium arch around stage frame

Tabs
Curtains that close across the stage

Iron
Fire curtain – usually only in professional venues

Cue
The line spoken before yours

Pyro
Pyrotechnics, flash pots, smoke and similar effects

Rake
The slope of the stage or floor of hall

Dry
Forgetting your lines

Corpse
Laugh uncontrollably

Dry ice
White "fog" effect

Blocking
Planning and agreeing moves during rehearsals

Setting up a Group

In this day and age stress is often part of our working lives.

Picture the following scene.

A long day at work, maybe full of problems, has finished. The journey home has been a pig, delays in traffic, bad weather, encouraging a nagging headache.

You arrive home late and without time to eat and shower, so you just shower, then it's back in the car and off to rehearsal.

At rehearsal you are expected to adopt a different persona whilst trying to remember perhaps several hundred words and what they mean.

Now do this two or three times a week for 7 or 8 weeks.

You may be forgiven for thinking this is a recipe for more stress or a free pass to a loony bin.

Actually the opposite is closer to reality – no really.

Honestly, it is a form of unwinding. Why?

Because it is totally different from work, it is with people who have a shared interest irrespective of job or background, and it is (or should be) with people you like and whose company you enjoy, which cannot always be said for those at work.

This social aspect is vitally important, after all fundamentally it is a hobby and must be enjoyable.

Rehearsals, although "hard work", should also be fun, but at the same time creative.

The work element is obviously necessary because the end result is a public performance for which people will have paid. They therefore have a right to expect a production of the highest possible standard. When this is achieved and the audience responds, the feeling of satisfaction is immense – indeed you are on a high without having taken anything!

Having been an active member of several groups and involved in productions over many years I would like to pass on the knowledge I have gained and share some of my experiences with you.

Non-professional theatre tends to attract a wide variety of characters, sometimes rather odd, sometimes eccentric and sometimes domineering.

I remember one group in East Anglia which had a particularly rigid format, meeting only when a production was planned, with no other activities. The committee – every group's nightmare – was ruled by a large, red-faced farmer who reminded me of Colonel Blimp. Whenever he was on stage he played himself, a large, red-faced, jovial, gin drinking character.

Talking of gin, I remember we did a production of *Not in the Book* by Arthur Watkin, a comedy thriller, with one of the characters played by a local chap called Frank. He also enjoyed his gin, usually in tumblers. In a tense moment in the action, the phone rings, and he was supposed to enter to ask who was calling. Under the influence of a considerable quantity of his chosen liquid, he jumped five pages and asked the question before the thing had rung. It is a nightmare situation of which more later on how to get out of it or, more importantly, how to avoid it.

Anyway I and two friends decided form a new group in the area.

The first question was where.

If you live in an urban area there may be several theatre clubs which will be supported by a potentially large audience. The public will also be well catered for by a variety of styles and probably a local professional company.

Villages are a different kettle of fish and may only be able to support one group. However there are often village halls with stages and activity rooms that are used by other groups.

Small villages are lovely in many ways but when thinking of a location you need to try and estimate the potential audience size.

Apart from family and friends, substantial other numbers are desirable, indeed necessary. After all, you will be aiming for a decent size audience over the course of three or four nights, not just one.

Why? Because a lot of work goes into it and to do it for only one night does not always seem worthwhile.

Our chosen village had a good village hall with a very good parking area at the rear and we all lived within a relatively short distance. So the group was born and was to run for around thirty years.

KEY POINTS

The amateur theatre group is a social group and must be democratic

It should aim for the highest possible standard

Pick a good location with adequate parking

Consider your audience/ the size of the area

The First Meeting

Where are you going to hold it?

This might seem obvious but it's actually very important and needs to be established right at the beginning before you start advertising and announcing the new society.

Remember at this point there is no money in the kitty – indeed there is not yet a kitty – so a room, if you hire one, needs to be very cheap.

Many pubs have rooms which local clubs of all sorts use for meetings and this may be a useful first line of enquiry. Prices vary but back rooms in pubs are often very cheap to hire for the evening because the landlord knows he will get extra customers.

If no such room exists, the local town or parish council might be able to help, although in my experience these people want payment in blood. Village halls sometimes have small back rooms which might be more reasonable but other local interest groups and clubs may have several dates already booked.

If all else fails you can hold the first meeting at home. However you should remember that whilst you obviously want a good turnout, if fifty potential members turn up can you cope?

You may think fifty is an optimistic number but we once advertised an audition for a pantomime and nearly sixty people turned up.

PUBLICITY

Deciding to form a theatre company is one thing, actually recruiting people is something else.

So having made the decision to form a group and booked a venue, you then draft and print your poster to be displayed in as many windows as possible.

This might seem daft, but put at least one poster upside down in a window: I guarantee people will stop and try to read it. They might think that someone has been stupid, but the point is it will be read.

Also don't forget the library. This again might seem obvious but recently in my area someone tried to start a poetry circle and wondered why not many people turned up. His poster went in the betting shop and a corner chippy. He forgot the library and bookshop which if you think about it would be seen by more people who might have been interested.

In this day and age with computers and high-quality printers it is easy to create eye-catching posters.

Essentially keep it clear and simple:

BE PART OF A NEW DRAMA GROUP
BECOME A LOCAL STAR
INTERESTED?
COME TO THE LAUNCH MEETING
AT ...
ON ...

PHONE OR EMAIL FOR DETAILS.
LOOK FORWARD TO SEEING YOU THERE.

Alternatively you could use the following which I once saw in a shop window in, of all places, Alaska.

WANTED – LAYABOUTS – LADIES OF ILL
REPUTE – DRUNKS – AND HAMS – FOR A
PRODUCTION OF
FIRST PIRATE'S DAUGHTER.

It certainly caught my eye and that is vital – it has to be eye-catching, and it was.

At this stage that is basically all you need. Unless of course you have already decided to put on a chosen play and you are advertising an audition.

A phone number and probably an email address should go on the poster in case a prospective member cannot attend the first meeting.

I suggest posters should go up about three weeks before the announced date to give people time to plan around other social activities. Don't forget to send a copy to your local press, radio and even TV station. If there is a college or upper school, send them one as well. You will need as wide an age spread as you can get.

Make sure you have a clear sense in your mind of what you expect or hope to achieve, assuming enough people turn up. You need to chair a business-like meeting. Yes I know it is only a hobby, but if twenty five people arrive each with an idea or opinion you must be able to control the meeting or nothing will get done.

THE MEETING

Okay so the day arrives and twenty five or more people turn up at your venue. It could be like a doctor's waiting room or just the opposite.

Before you formally start, introduce a few people to each other and before long the ice will be broken.

Declare the meeting open and introduce yourself, your reasons for the gathering, your hopes and objectives, maybe past experience in theatre, then invite each person to introduce themselves, and as they do so pass a sheet of paper around so a record of names and contact details are collected.

From this introduction will or may emerge a wide range of experiences, interests, talent indicators and abilities.

Open the discussion and get everyone's ideas on what they would like to do.

It is almost certain that some of those who turn up will have some past experience. This is the wealth of your new group. In addition someone who paints, does woodwork as a hobby, or is competent with electrics or dressmaking is as important as someone who may have stage experience.

In any group of people a leader will emerge almost naturally, but this leader, who may also direct, must have a clear objective, which should be a production of the highest possible standard from everybody's point of view and that includes the audience.

Remember they are paying good money for the privilege of seeing us "do our thing". So however modest a production, it costs money to get in, and for retired couples who will probably make up a significant percentage of the audience, it may represent a good chunk of their leisure fund.

Why are you holding the first meeting? If it is to create a new theatre group, try and make the positive move of deciding on a play and if possible find a director.

Obviously some people prefer comedy to drama whilst others would like to do pantomime. In our group we did three shows a year, one of each, generally in April, October and the end of January.

If you set up the meeting with the intention of directing the first production, get a set of books of the play from the library and have a read through. It will stimulate interest and also perhaps give you a clue on how people sound.

Another job on the first evening is to select a secretary, treasurer and publicity officer. I am not a lover of committees but these three are essential.

Once a production has been decided and agreed, it will need to be advertised, so a publicity officer is vital and should cover all issues related to marketing, public relations, sponsorships and advertising; in fact, he or she may additionally head up capital campaigns or other fundraising events. Thus, it's necessary that this person be a dynamic visionary who gets the job done. An introvert usually does not do well as an amateur dramatic society's publicity officer, as he or she will need to network as part of his or her responsibility.

An Important Aside: Please remember that just as every person is unique, so is every amateur dramatics society. Therefore, yours may need to arrange roles differently than outlined above. Still, the aforementioned positions are those regularly found among groups

It is also advisable to have a production target date although this will depend upon venue availability. So, for example, if this first meeting is in June, it would be good to aim for say October. Why?

If a date is agreed – a deadline if you like – more effort will emerge to make it happen.

Once the group is formed, set up monthly meetings. In our group we picked the second Thursday in each month so people could plan many months ahead.

If nothing else, they are great social evenings with everybody getting to know each other. These sessions can also be used for play readings or improvisation games and specific character analysis.

KEY POINTS

Publicity matters – consider all options
Cover all local media
Keep the poster simple
Plan the meeting – what are you going to talk about
Do not dictate but outline your vision
Appoint Secretary, Treasurer and Publicity officer
Make introductions get to know the strengths and interests of the group
Decide on a direction and date
Agree and fix date of second meeting

Raising Money

Unfortunately even in the tranquil world of Amateur Theatre (if you believe that you'll believe anything!) money raises its ugly head. Funds will be needed from the word go. Starting an amateur dramatic society is exciting, but without a doubt, it can be challenging to find the money to fund it and then keep it running.

Indeed you may have already spent some money on posters advertising your new group and the first meeting. Unless you are rich or have a wealthy benefactor you will have to raise funds one way or another.

Since the curse of the boot sale blighted our countryside, jumble sales have become less viable and now do not raise what they used to a few years ago, but it is a useful start.

Your local council will probably have an art sector and this avenue should be looked into as it may be possible to get a grant.

Some groups I have known have an annual membership fee of a few pounds. This obviously helps with upfront costs. For example, if about thirty people turn up and agree to join and also agree a membership fee of say £20 a year, it will set up a kitty straight away, worth a potential £600. It also shows commitment of the members to the new group.

Obviously the group will need a bank account in the name of the group which will require at least two signatures for cheques.

Why do you need cash so soon? If nothing else at this stage, cash will be needed to pay – hopefully only a small amount – the venue where you are holding your meetings.

Once a play is decided upon and a date fixed, a performance licence will have to be applied and paid for, although this can wait until nearer the time, along will other things which are dealt with later.

Many groups hold fundraising events in order to pay their production costs which will include set and costume pieces, and perhaps a storage room, stage rental charges, marketing, advertising and so forth. Such events can be of any shape or form, from sales of food to "free" performances where audience donations are requested. Generally speaking, annual fundraisers can be a nice way to add a few coins to your society's coffers, but they typically won't cover all expenses for the year.

Radio stations, financial institutions and other corporate entities are often willing to "underwrite" a show or two for an amateur dramatics group. Sponsorships of this type can run the gamut as far as amounts go and are very dependent on the plays you produce, your society's locale and the sponsoring business.

For example, if you are in Essex, i.e. Matthew Hopkins the Witchfinder General county and your group is planning to stage *The Crucible* by Arthur Miller, a play based on the Salem witch trials in 1692, next season, your neighbourhood firms may agree to sponsor the show. The most important aspect to remember about sponsorship is that you need to continuously thank those who have contributed and give them publicity in the production programme.

KEY POINTS

Agree an annual membership fee
Hold fundraising events to help with publicity
Persuade a local business to sponsor your group

Production Venue

When you have decided to put on a theatrical production a stage can be useful, you may laugh at that but it is not essential. I have seen plays acted out very well in the corner of a pub bar. A clear space is the only necessity. However, when starting up it is probably easier to work on stage, although this may depend on the experience of some of your group members.

So where do you find one?

Schools and village halls immediately come to mind. Most schools have a stage but the problem might be the availability of "backstage" space, including dressing rooms which might be very small or non-existent. In addition there is the fact that it may only be available during school holidays.

Villages tend to have community halls and such like but they will be used by many other local clubs and societies and as a result are often booked up several months ahead. There are six essential features to look for when choosing a production venue:

    A.   THE STAGE
    B.   WING AND BACKSTAGE SPACE.
    C.   LIGHTING/ELECTRICS
    D.   DRESSING ROOM FACILITIES
    E.   REASONABLE AUDIENCE SPACE AND COMFORT.
    F.   KITCHEN

The Stage

What is a reasonable size is a matter of opinion. I have seen productions of genius on a square handkerchief and near disasters on huge stages. The thing to remember is not to choose a production with major amounts of furniture if the stage area is not very big.

Keep it simple, especially your first production.

Obviously the space will influence the design of the set and the amount of furniture you can use. A settee and a couple of chairs will fill some stages. You might therefore be restricted to some extent regarding scene changes on a conventional set but most village halls and school stages are workable.

At the front of the stage there will be the proscenium arch – the pros. The curtain or tabs will usually pull across behind the pros. When closed there may well be three or four feet of stage before the edge. This space can be used for announcements or action while the set is being changed.

One factor over which you have no control is the height of the ceiling above the stage. Professionally known as "fly space", if the height is really good it will be possible to "drop" effects that may highlight a scene, such as stardust in a pantomime for example. Props can also be lowered in if it suits the production. There will also probably be facilities above the stage for fixing, or "rigging" lights. If the venue is used regularly lights may already be in place.

Some stages may have a very slight slope down towards the audience. Known as "the rake" this may affect decisions about furniture on wheels.

If you are really lucky there may well be a trapdoor in the centre of the stage. Advantages can be twofold. Firstly, and perhaps most likely, it would be used in a pantomime where characters can appear and disappear. The other advantage is

that there will be storage space under the stage which can be
used for scenery at the end of the run.

KEY POINTS

If stage area is small choose a simple set.
Tailor your set to the stage area.
Use the stage area to your advantage.

Backstage and Wing space

We can adapt to the size of the stage but the benefits of "wing" space cannot be overemphasised.

The "wings" refers to the space "offstage" at either side of the acting area. The wings house the prompt, often the lighting and sound controls, and depending upon the space, additional scenery, props and anything else needed during performance.

In addition, the space will be needed by someone waiting for their cue to come on during a performance.

In reality, the wings in village halls and the like are usually very narrow, so it is essential that they be kept clear of everything that is not required for the show.

These areas must also be kept as dark as possible as any light will "spill" on to the stage and at the very least will be a distraction for both cast and audience.

In an ideal world there will usually be access to the rooms behind the stage from the wings on each side to give an easy path to and from the dressing rooms.

If you are lucky you will also have a backstage area for additional storage but many halls do not have this.

KEY POINTS

Keep wings clear and dark.
If a choice of venues is possible, go for good wing space and backstage area.

Dressing Room

Most village halls or community centres will only have a single area to change in, do make-up and so on.

If the thought of several people of both sexes in various stages of undress in one room bothers you, stick to stamp collecting.

The reality in my experience is that nobody takes any notice of anyone else – they're too busy getting ready to go on stage, thinking about their character, what their opening line is and getting it right when they get there.

There is always the option of having the make-up table across the centre of the area so all the men are on one side and the ladies the other.

You will also need to set aside a corner of the dressing room for youngsters under chaperone laws, although their parents will probably be in the show as well.

If you have a large cast with several costume changes, in a pantomime for instance, the dressing room mid-performance will probably be chaotic, so organisation and the provision of clothes rails will be essential. You can often get clothes rails from shops that are upgrading their equipment. But clarity of space and discipline are very important.

A good size mirror will be needed along with a basic kit of stage make-up or "slap" as it is generally known. In modern plays however make-up is less important than when doing Shakespeare or a pantomime for example.

PROPS

Another essential element is the "props" table. This will house items used by the cast on stage, so they must be readily available.

Whether cups, glasses, dummy pistols or magic wands, props should be laid out on the table and ideally a felt tip pen should be used to draw around them. That way it will be immediately obvious if something is missing.

Occasionally a cast member might forget to take a prop with them when they go on stage. This can be very awkward, depending upon the scene. I remember one occasion when we did a pantomime, one of the characters edged towards prompt corner and whispered, "I forgot my magic potion, can you get it for me." The prompt quickly and quietly went down into the dressing room, retrieved it and then slid it on to the stage so the actor could "discover it". Fortunately no prompt was needed during those few moments.

Another important thing to remember is noise. Once the performance has started it is essential to keep quiet in the dressing room as the sound in some halls may well be heard by the audience, not to mention the cast on stage. So a ban on mobile phones backstage and in the dressing room is most essential.

KEY POINTS

Organise space
Use a good size mirror for the "slap"
Prepare the "prop" table
Keep quiet once show starts

Lighting and Sound

Without lighting, no stage play can be seen, so somebody with knowledge of electrics is always a valuable member.

"Sparks" usually assists in rigging the sound as well.

These days there are many control panels and systems available, so if it is more convenient, lighting and sound can be controlled from the rear of the hall. This can be an advantage because whoever is running the system has total visual access to the production.

It is likely that an existing stage in a village hall or school will already have some basic lighting units. All lights must be both clamped and chained to overhead bars.

Once rehearsals are underway for a production the units may need to be adjusted to the correct angle to meet the needs of the storyline.

Sometimes a "follow" spot may be needed. This will usually be done by hand from the rear of the hall.

Many village halls have speakers to which a sound system can be connected. Whilst straight plays do not need mics on stage it may be useful to have one so announcements can be made from backstage or in the wings before the performance starts. For example, "Ladies and Gentlemen welcome to tonight's performance which will commence in five minutes."

In addition, in some scripts, usually comedies, there may well be a VO – voice off – with a few lines coming into the story without a "body". This will be via a mic from someone in the wings.

In pantomimes music is essential. This may be either a prerecorded soundtrack, a live keyboard player, or if you are really lucky a trio or even a quartet.

When I have "done the music" for pantos I have set my keyboard up at the back of the hall and so have had a complete view of the action which for me was essential.

In my opinion playing live music adds more atmosphere to a performance than using a prerecorded CD, so if you have a keyboard player or other musicians in the group it is a bonus. In addition it has been known for the wrong track on a CD to be cued against a song. Where live music is used this is extremely unlikely to happen.

KEY POINTS

Make sure lamps are clamped and hooked
Ensure there are up-to-date checks on all electrics
If possible get live music

Your Audience

By definition a village hall is geared for public use and adequate seating is usually available. School halls are different – especially if it is a junior or infant school with very small chairs or benches which are certainly not very comfortable for adults.

Either way, the number of seats will be determined by the fire regulations, which will take into consideration the floor area and number of existing fire exits.

If possible it is a good idea to have a drinks counter – if only tea or coffee. It does bring in a bit of extra money and helps with the interval.

It is an obvious thing to mention, but by taking care of your audience with the environment, refreshments and, above all, the best production you can present, the more likely you are to see them back again and again.

As a change from the usual rows of seats, you can set up tables of six or eight seats, invite the audience to bring nibbles and drinks and create more of a party atmosphere. This works especially well with a lighthearted play or comedy evening.

KEY POINTS

Try to ensure audience comfort
Do an evening around tables
Offering refreshments can be a good way of raising a bit of extra money and ensuring audience comfort.

Who Directs

In many groups the director volunteers, but not in all.

I once visited a group in the north of England and learned that they had a play reading and casting committee who, once the play was chosen, then picked the director. I find that very strange and for my money totally unacceptable.

Essentially the director must really want to do the play, must have a feeling about the subject or the characters, and have a clear vision of how he or she wants it to look. This is why two separate productions of the same script can often turn out to be so very different.

Although he or she will have a vision of how it should look, the director should not stop cast members making suggestions. Some may work, others may not, but directors should at least listen and, if nothing else, it will get support from the cast

Directing can be a difficult and demanding role but one filled with satisfaction. To see a play come together on the first night in the way you imagined it really can give you a high.

One thing is essential: the director must have the respect and total support of all involved in the production if it is to be successful.

If not, find someone else.

We all have stresses and strains in life but we must not take them to rehearsal. It is after all a hobby and must be enjoyable.

I remember one particular production whose director was overbearing and rude almost continually, so much so that when I arrived for a rehearsal one evening early in the schedule my head was bitten off. I rejoined that if her tone was going to continue I would go home. The answer was that she did not care, so I left and went home – for the first and only time in my life I had walked out of a rehearsal.

When I turned up for the next one she had calmed down and things improved. It was a shame because all the cast were accomplished and the eventual production was very good. It was however not a happy one.

It is possible that within a new group there will be at least one person who has had some previous experience at directing and it will make sense for that individual to take the reins for the first effort.

However, your "experienced" volunteer could be a disaster.

A certain group took part in a national event on one occasion and a member agreed to direct. He even went away on a sponsored director's workshop for a weekend. The result was a near-disaster simply because he failed in his duty to the production. He obviously had learned nothing about directing.

When you take on a play in whatever capacity it must take priority of your spare time for the few weeks involved. If you are not prepared for it to do so, don't do it.

So having volunteered as director, head for the library and pick maybe half a dozen scripts of the agreed style, i.e. comedy, drama etc., taking note of the numbers of cast required.

Also think about character age. Whether it is a drama or a farce, if the characters are all residents of an old folks' home for example, can you cast it if all the members of your group are in their twenties or thirties? Unfortunately, physical age is a factor that is frequently overlooked in some local groups but it is obviously very important.

In professional productions you may well see an actor or actress playing a character that is thirty years older than they are. It works because they are "in the business" and have been professionally trained. With am-dram groups it may not work so well, so when casting try to get the age of the person who is playing the role much closer to that of the character.

When you have gathered together potential scripts, slowly go through them all, discarding them until your chosen one is decided.

<u>*CHARACTER*</u>

So both the play and the director have been chosen, now comes – no not casting, but homework for the director.

Before casting, he or she must know the play very well indeed. It should not be a case of "Professional man thirtyish. Elderly woman with walking stick. Okay that's Bill and Wendy."

Indeed, the director must read between the lines and decide how he wants the character to sound-: timid, aggressive, sexy or a classical sound, and how the character looks-; shy, overbearing, frightened, confident, disinterested or a professional manner, for example.

Age and experience can be adjusted to some extent with costumes and make-up but for amateurs the voice may be more difficult. Few have had any kind of voice or speech training.

If the character has been to Eton or some other high-profile public school it is unlikely he would speak like a cockney. Equally, the opposite is true.

These points are obvious but sometimes overlooked. On the other hand the play may be geographically re-sited: the plot and action may be in London but if the group is in Liverpool it may be just as easily set in Penny Lane as Petticoat lane, depending of course on the story ingredients.

<u>*SCRIPT*</u>

Obviously each member of the cast needs a copy of the script and several other copies will be required for the crew, including the director and the prompt.

Even when library copies are used, it is worth buying some copies for breaking down and marking up. A good idea is to carefully take out the pages of the script and place them in a ring binder with a blank sheet of paper opposite each page. This allows you to read the script and make notes alongside it that can easily be viewed.

Now the work begins. I would suggest that you read the script at least a dozen times and begin to visualise the stage action. The more you read it the clearer the picture you will have of the characters and your ideas for casting will begin to emerge.

Think about what you are aiming for and try and "hear" the words on the page. Certainly most modern plays are identifiable in terms of the characters and storyline and by picturing the scenes in your mind it will help you decide which play to do.

Voice, appearance and facial expression, to name but a few, will begin to point you towards particular group members for casting.

This is another reason why the director should have read the script at least a dozen times before casting and rehearsals starts.

If you are doing a three-act play, do not expect to get through it in an evening, at least for the first few sessions (this is apart from the early read-through).

It is far better to work the acts per evening – so for example, Tuesday do act one and Thursday act two and so on. This way it may also give some of the cast the night off now and again because they may not all appear in all of the acts.

KEY POINTS

Director must be totally committed
Director must have total understanding of the script.
Choose the script carefully based on your group members
Director should read it many times before first group reading and visualise the characters.

Types of Play

A drama can be a murder story, a thriller or just a serious story about the relationships between people.

However, some drama scripts may need extra sound or lighting effects to create a certain atmosphere. In addition, a nasty character must be cast with care. "Atmosphere" is everything when creating a nasty or serious scene. It really matters, so when doing a serious play think about mannerisms, gestures and facial expressions. They all add to the character, especially a "nasty" one.

How different when doing a comedy. It is perhaps a mistake to think comedy is easier to do than drama. In fact, the opposite is true. With comedy timing is so important. Think of your favourite comedy on TV or perhaps one you have seen on stage. The pauses and facial expressions can make or break it.

Vocal inflections can often make a difference between a "straight" line and a funny one.

Think also of the eyes. A good example would be Manuel from *Fawlty Towers*. His eyes were all over the place which added a great deal to his character.

Take another step and think of farce. Of the three, comedy, drama and farce, farce is the most difficult to do. Why? Because timing is critical in performance and the pace is often faster. The lines, movement, reaction, body language and facial expressions are important in any production but in a farce the tempo is greater, so accuracy is critical.

Think again of *Fawlty Towers*, of the speed and reaction of one character to another.

There is no doubt that doing a farce is great fun but it does take a lot of work.

Of course there is one genre that I have not mentioned and that is pantomime. Whilst pantos vary widely both from other genres and amongst themselves, they are essentially family entertainment. It is both an introduction for youngsters as performers and spectators and whilst the former builds self-confidence, the latter encourages an interest in arts and culture.

In many plays, sets can be almost non-existent but in a panto they are arguably essential. So a lot more set design, painting and construction will be needed.

There will also be a difference in casting. Very often, younger family members will be required in the show. Obviously there is no age limit, but when my drama group did a panto we had cast members as young as six up to well into their teens.

The benefits of this to the youngsters can be significant.

I remember a friend joined us to appear in a panto. At the time he was on some educational committees and when the show was over and done he said he had never seen a group of youngsters with such self-confidence, which was gained from teamwork and appearing on stage.

In addition to creating a set, costumes are needed. These can be hired of course but again that is an expense. So if you have a member who is a skilled seamstress, this is a huge advantage.

Also a panto almost always has music and songs. It is easy to prerecord a CD with the chosen numbers but if you can get live music it is so much better.

A modern keyboard has a great many "instruments" and rhythms plus some weird and wonderful sound effects in addition to a piano sound.

However, for a newly formed group a musical may be too ambitious, but if several of your new members have experience in this area then why not. One thing is for sure. A musical takes more planning and rehearsal time than a straight play. In addition, if there are dance numbers, a choreographer will be needed to work out the dance routines, which in turn will require music.

Another line to follow could be doing an evening of sketches, either comic or serious. Generally these will have little or no set, often a small cast in each piece, so more roles to play for everyone in the group.

KEY POINTS

Choose a play everyone is comfortable with
Consider the different requirements of each genre i.e. acting skills, cast, music, set
Pick a production that is not too complex in set etc

Scripts – Where to Look

Assuming you have no preconceived idea on a title, start at the local library. Each county library system has certain branches that have specialist collections. A phone call or a check online will ascertain the location of the branch holding the drama collection. This will run into several hundred titles, with complete sets of scripts for many. Nowadays a computer in the library will identify plays according to specific categories, length, and numbers of characters of each sex.

One major source of scripts is of course the publisher Samuel French who specialise in just that, but there are other publishers that can be found online.

It will be necessary, before you choose, to know how many people you have on your acting strength. Of the first meeting of twenty five you may only have perhaps half that number who actually want to go on stage.

Strictly speaking you should only choose a play because you want to do it but the reality in amateur circles is that you are governed by available numbers. For example it would be difficult to do *The Devil's Disciple* by George Bernard Shaw, which has around a dozen in the cast, if you only have two men and two women.

The best thing to do if you do not have a play in mind is to invite members to obtain a script of their choice, take out several from the library and hold a series of readings. It is a good way to spend an evening, you get to hear everyone and the more you read the more you get a feel for a good script.

Perhaps start with some one-act plays which may take thirty or forty minutes, as opposed to a major three-act script which may take well over a couple of hours.

KEY POINTS

Know the acting strength within the group
Read several scripts
Try different styles
Read out loud and bring it to life

Choosing a Play

The venue, stage and the availability of the necessary facilities will all be factors in the decision regarding which script or type of show is chosen. A pantomime for example generally has much more scenery than perhaps a straight play.

So a useful consideration for your new group's first production is perhaps to pick a play where there are no major set changes, apart from perhaps moving some furniture about.

If the play has more than one set, "the change" will have to be readily available, so "wing space" and back stage access will be a significant advantage.

Sets cost money to build of course, which is another factor to be considered.

Quite apart from practicalities, cost will be part of the equation, particularly if your production happens to be a costume drama, unless of course you are brilliant with a sewing machine.

So your choice of first production should take into account several factors, some artistic, some practical and some financial.

Selling tickets for performances is the way most societies make ends meet. But beware – if the plays you offer are forgettable, you may have difficulty getting people in the seats.

Consequently, it will be a good idea to offer the public quality titles at least for the first year or two. After that hopefully you will have attracted a steady "base" of supporters who will be more likely to support you when you throw an "unconventional" production into the mix once in a while.

Not all productions need elaborate sets or costume changes, so as I said the first production should be kept simple and not too technical – and if the script is good and the cast really work at it, it should be a success.

So talking of simple sets, take for example the following extract from one of my sketches called the "Turner Prize".

 Interview on TV talkshow.

Joe   *Watcha mates sorry that Parky can't be here tonight but I'm a brilliant stand-in for him. I'm only joking – No really I'm Joe King.*
The first thing we are going to talk about is the latest showing of the 3rd age movement at the Cutpurse Gallery which I was forced to go and see last week. To discuss it I am joined in the studio by er (drops notes on floor – gathers them up while moaning) oh hell sorry er half a mo ah yes –
Huge Perciman-Smythe, art critic of the Preposterous Quarterly and doyen of the 3rd age movement. At least that's what it says here.

(Enter Hughe)
Greetings Huge nice to see you.

Hughe   *Hughe.*

Joe   *Pardon*

Hughe   *Hughe – my name is Hughe, darling, not Huge.*

Joe   *Oh so sorry mate.*

Hughe   *Well normally I would be delighted to be here but really the colour co-ordination in this new studio – well my dear it does leave one – well disorientated don't you know.*

Joe   *Yes well no doubt them makeover people did their rehearsal in here. But anyway tell us about this latest controversial exhibition at* *the Cutpurse Gallery which I've been told contains a contender for the Turner Prize.*

Hughe   *Well you call it controversial. But I of course do not agree. But whether it is or not – is in the intellect of the sapiens who have the wit to consider it.*

Joe   *Sorry – sapien. What are you on about?*

Hughe   *My dear man (patronising) Sapiens – Homo sapiens – you and me.*

Joe   *Here just a minute who are you calling a homo?*

Hughe   *Homo! Homo sapiens – mankind – all of us.*

Joe   *So not Queer then?*

Hughe   *(very camp) Queer – my dear CERTAINLY NOT.*

You can see that from this short extract the only staging that is needed is a table, a couple of chairs and some paper which is dropped on the "studio" floor.

So very simple to stage.

Possibly the style of show which needs the most staging with props and effects is a pantomime.

With pantomimes, costumes are vital and usually a group will hire the more elaborate ones, but again it is an added cost.

Other shows such as straight comedy or drama may or may not need elaborate scenery but even here things can be made simple. The performance essentially depends firstly upon a good script, secondly a dedicated cast and thirdly a thoroughly committed director who knows what they are doing and has a strong feeling for the script. If these are in place it could be argued that a set is almost irrelevant.

There are specialist publishers for acting material who have lists available in all categories. They are also able to give advice regarding genre and things like staging difficulties.

Of course not all productions have to be a two or three-act play. There are many one-act play festivals around the country where perhaps three or four groups will each do a short piece of maybe thirty or thirty five minutes. The advantage here is that it takes less time to rehearse and usually has only a very simple set and few if any props.

Finally when deciding to do a particular play bear in mind that although you may have enough people to cast all the characters, is anyone left for the many other jobs that need to be done? Such as stage crew, prompt, costumes, front of house, publicity and tea and coffee making.

The backstage and front of house activities, as well as the role of director, are dealt with in more detail elsewhere in this guide. However, it is important that these roles are factored in when choosing a play.

KEY POINTS

Consider stage size
Keep first production simple
Consider production style
Consider available cast

Performance Licence

In general terms it is now necessary to obtain a licence from the local town or borough council when a public performance is to be staged even though it may be on or in private premises.

The licence covers all types of show and the authority will usually require at least a month's notice, although some may process it quicker. It will be an 'occasional 'licence for which there is no standard format.

Contact your local council office and they will give help and advice and also present you with a questionnaire to complete. Things like what will the event be, dates and times. In addition confirmation of general health and Safety awareness, capacity numbers and whether or not any pyrotechnics will be used.

The reason for the licence is covered in the Theatres Act 1968. It covers things like fire, health and safety, the number of exits, the maximum audience numbers and fireproofing of scenery if necessary.

In addition you may need permission to perform the script from the author or publisher, after all, the writer earns royalties from performance.

As an example of costs, the following are from Samuel French as applicable in 2013. The royalty fee is per performance – that is each night. Each play has a code in the front of the scripts which relate to performing rights.

Code A = £10.00
Code B = £18.00
Code C = £32.00
Code D = £37.00
Code E = £43.00
Code F = £48.00
Code G = £48.00

Code H = £70.00
Code J = £70.00
Code K = £80.00
Code L = £88.00
Code M = £93.00

A-G are one-act plays
H-M are full length

You should be able to get the relevant information from the publisher of the script you are using. Remember that no part of any script can legally be performed publicly without permission.

In addition where music is used, in a pantomime or musical for example, a fee may be required where a public performance is given.

A good source for information is the Performing Rights Society in the UK.

KEY POINTS

Check with your local council office over obtaining a performance licence

Check with script publisher with regard to royalties and fees

Play Readings

Regular play readings should form part of the group's activities. These can be fun, especially when the selection is a good comedy or farce, and they give the group a greater awareness of what is on the library shelves.

Also, reading a script out loud gives it life, which reading in silence does not.

The more readings you do helps the group decide whether they would prefer to do light or heavier material.

You will also find that some members have a natural flair for the funny line, others for the dramatic.

Some people find reading cold difficult but being a bad reader is no indication that the individual is a bad actor. The opposite can in fact be true.

Another advantage of reading is that prospective directors get some idea of what everybody sounds like in different characters and accents. Also different scripts require different paces when reading. Scripts only come alive when read out loud, with various dialects and changing pace.So armed with the knowledge of possible cast members the director is better equipped to choose his or her production.

Essentially, play readings should be enjoyable. They can be done more or less anywhere, but if you have the space to experiment with moves it is much more valuable.

One good way of approaching play readings is to take a short section – perhaps a scene or two – and read it through two or three times at a different pace. Then by discussion, speeches can be analysed to find out what is between the lines.

If time is short just read the first act. This should be enough to give you an impression of the characters, setting and so on.

Actually reading the play aloud will give you a rough idea of how long the performance will take. For example, if the actual cold reading time exclusive of coffee breaks etc is about an hour and a half, it is probable that the performance will take around two hours or perhaps a shade longer, allowing for an interval of fifteen or twenty minutes. So an ideal length for an evening's show.

Above all, play readings in a new group help everybody gain confidence and create the feeling of a team. And of course working as a team is 100% necessary.

KEY POINTS

Get everyone to choose a script to read
Do regular readings
Try dialects, accents pace and mood

Chaperones

Unfortunately in this day and age youngsters are not as "free" as their parents were when they were young.

Because of some nasty events in recent years, a new law was introduced requiring school-age children up to and including Year 11 to be chaperoned. Those who are taking part in, or rehearsing for, a public performance must by law be accompanied by a registered chaperone, that is if they cannot be accompanied by their parents or carer.

Basically the law states that a chaperone can supervise a maximum of 12 children at a time, who must all be of the same sex. The chaperone is responsible for the child at all times except when they are actively rehearsing, performing or with a parent or carer.

In reality, youngsters in an Amateur Theatre group are unlikely to be there without parents or very close family friends, so personally I do not, and certainly never have seen, a problem. But it is something that groups need to be aware of and ensure that the correct rules are followed for any younger performers.

KEY POINTS:

Ensure the correct procedures are followed for any younger performers

Casting

Forget all the jokes you may have heard about the casting couch, it might happen in Hollywood but not in the non-professional theatre. If it does I have never seen it, however casting meetings are essential to the development of the play and can often produce surprises.

Copies of scripts should go out to anyone who is interested in reading for a part before the casting evening. It is after all only fair and in the interest of the production that they come prepared.

One thing is for sure – you will not go through the whole piece on a casting evening. As director you will have read the script a few times so for each character pick a page or a scene that brings out their emotion, anger or mood. Get the actors to go through these sections and you should begin to have a good idea for casting.

What you are looking for as director will be clearer if you have read your chosen script several times. If you have, it will actually make casting easier, assuming of course you have enough people.

What I look for in the first instance when I am directing is a particular sound, feeling or emotion in the voice.

On one occasion I directed a production of *Pack of Lies* by Hugh Whitemore, a play about the 1960s spies Peter and Helen Kroger.

We came to the casting evening which I approached with a completely open mind as to who would play each part. I had, however, been through the script several times so I had a clear picture of what I wanted. I had a specific idea about the character, Mrs. Jackson, which is the largest part in the play.

Several people read for it but I soon realised that the sound – the voice, feeling and emotion – I wanted came from a lady who had very little experience, yet there was a certain depth in her voice which told me that she well understood what she was reading, she was absolutely correct. Unfortunately there was another member who really wanted the role. She was upset at not getting it but she simply wasn't right.

As it turned out my chosen member was excellent and had a very good press review.

People often come to auditions with high expectations and they may well be disappointed but that is the way it turns out. If a couple of people seem equal get them to talk in depth about how they see the role or character. This will help you decided who is right for the part.

In addition the director may often be faced with two alternatives. Either six people turn up for twelve parts or the reverse. Either way there are sometimes difficult decisions to be made.

When I am casting a production I obviously have to take into account size and age but fundamentally I look for a vocal inflection – a feeling and emotion for what is being said.

Of course it is very tempting to go for the actor or actress in the group who has the most experience and automatically give them the main part. However this may not necessarily be what you are looking for and it does not give new members a fair chance or encourage them to stay with the group.

If you are lucky enough to have a choice of people for a play, someone is going to be disappointed, but choices have to be made.

If you are going to audition for a part, it pays to have read it through a few times and ideally at least a couple of times out loud – yes out loud. The only way to get any idea of what the dialogue sounds like is to recite it. A script only comes alive when spoken out loud. More on the benefit of this later when we discuss learning lines.

The important factor to remember is, don't audition if you are not prepared to attend all rehearsals. Obviously the unexpected crops up and you miss one, but to say, "I can only do every other one," is letting everyone down and simply is not good enough.

When a character is missing from rehearsal it can make things very difficult for the others. It is after all a team effort.

There is no room for "stars" in amateur theatre. Across all the productions I have been involved in, I have directed, acted, helped paint the set, made the tea and been front of house, and that is how it should be.

TIME FRAME

Inevitably rehearsal schedules need to be discussed at the casting meeting. We all have jobs to do and different nights suit different people. A vote on which nights to rehearse is probably the best, although it may depend on the availability of the rehearsal room.

It is essential to agree a start time – and very important to stick to it.

So often rehearsals that are scheduled for say eight pm do not start until ten, fifteen or even twenty minutes later. Add together these missing minutes and over the run of rehearsals you will have probably wasted at least two evenings which have had to be paid for if you are hiring a room. Remember, if someone turns up late without good reason, it holds everybody up, and is plain bad manners.

Once the play is cast it is a good idea to spend the first couple of sessions just sitting around the table and reading it through out loud. After a couple of read-throughs you should find that the characters begin slowly to emerge. This helps everyone get a full understanding of the "behind the scenes" story and a greater clarity of the part they are going to play.

KEY POINTS

When choosing an actor to play a role look for a sound and feeling
Be open-minded when choosing a cast.
Select the actor who suits the vision of the play and character rather than simply the most experienced.
Insist on total commitment from your cast
Ensure that rehearsals start on time

Text Analysis

The first two evenings at least will require the attendance of all the cast and ideally the stage crew.

These two sessions and possibly more are ideally held round a table for total read-throughs.

For the stage crew, it will begin to highlight any action regarding set changes as the story unfolds, also lighting, sound, and any effects that they need to get hold of.

Close study of the text is also required by the cast as the director begins to explain his feeling about the characters and what he is aiming for.

There may be specific references in the dialogue such as, "I saw a tall man etc, that's him," This again comes back to casting. Credibility will be lost if the person being pointed at is only 5'4"Or maybe something more in depth is required, such as a deep but subtle change in facial expressions or body language when a character hears of some dark deed.

This kind of detail can only be gained by a director who goes through the text several times with care. Most, if not all plays can be broken down into segments, perhaps a particular scene, exchange or topic in the script. This may be as little as half a page containing a certain mood change or action. These short sections need to be identified if possible before casting because when hearing people read for a particular part they will be convenient chunks for a busy audition.

GET INSIDE THE CHARACTER

These extracts may be just a phrase within a sentence but could highlight a change in character, mood or intention. Certainly close study also helps the cast identify themselves in the play and how they relate to the other characters.

Above all get the cast to portray their characters in a way that makes the play work and brings out the story in depth.

If any cast members are not feeling comfortable get them to try different improvisation exercises to get them focused and put the rhythm of the play back on track.

By now you are beginning to experiment with pauses – they lend emphasis to what comes next – inflection, possible accents, and trying to get into the mind of the role.

Yes, early days, but this is where it starts.

If you look at a page in a script and read it from the top – slowly – you will find in most cases that a certain word or line on that page changes the flow, mood or course of action or character. This may in turn change the tempo of the scene or "position" of the character.

Identify that point and others like it and the production will be the better for it.

Take the following example from one of my sketches. It is a scene in an old folks' home where Edna who is a new resident, goes into the lounge and sits in the empty chair. Jodie is the carer.

This sketch takes place in the lounge of an old folks' home. So a few 'old' characters are dotted about in chairs staring into space – the occasional groan may be heard. TV is on in the corner. As the tabs open an elderly lady – Edna – on a Zimmer frame approaches a chair.

She sits

EDNA	*Good morning.*
	(nobody answers – some look)
	(enter Jodie – carer)
JODIE	*Hello my dears everybody okay today?*
	(no answer)
	Oh that's good. It's a lovely morning.
EDNA	*Yes it is.*
JODIE	*Hello Edna how are you settling in?*
EDNA	*Very well thank you*
GLADYS	*(sitting in corner)*
	She's sitting in my chair
JODIE	*Gladys what is the matter dear?*

GLADYS	*She's in my chair.*
JODIE	*Oh well it doesn't really matter does it?*
GLADYS	*I was going to sit there but she got there first. (points at Mary)*
JODIE	*Well I expect Edna picked the empty one dear. (she sighs)*
MARY	*She is mixed up again.*
JODIE	*Yes Mary I am sure she is.*
MARY	*Peter can you get me a taxi, I must get to the station. My Fred's coming home today – I'll just get my coat.*
GLADYS	*You shut up you silly old woman. Why don't you shut up – you're always going on.*
JODIE	*(under breath) Seconds out round 2 – here we go again. (Louder) ladies ladies (quieter) the vicar will be here soon for our little service.*
EDNA	*Are we having a service?*
JODIE	*Every Wednesday at about 11-00*
EDNA	*Why Wednesday – it should be Sunday shouldn't it?*

Mary is clearly "losing it" and thinks that Fred is coming home but in fact he was killed in the war.

Gladys tells her to shut up – so the lines show the frustration from those in the home towards Mary. Many scenes have keywords or phrases and by searching for them and dissecting the action around them your production will be much better so text analysis is vital for a good production.

KEY POINTS

Read closely
Read "in between the lines"
"Learn" your character
Pick up key phrases that may change the pace or mood

Becoming the Character

Of vital importance – and the credibility of the production depends on it – is the task of learning to be the character, not just reciting the lines.

Any professional acting school will, amongst other things, teach you the three golden rules of character creation. Three questions that you must ask of the role you are going to play are:

1   Who am I?
2   What do I want?
3   How do I get it?

Who Am I

Many scripts give an outline of a character. For example;-

Peter – A local solicitor who has a serious cough

That's fine and helps casting, but if 'Peter' is a middle-aged solicitor or perhaps even a detective inspector he wouldn't normally be played by a twenty year old.

So often amateur productions are spoiled simply because the director and actors have not discussed, at all, let alone in depth, the character in question.

So again I emphasise the importance of the director going through the script several times before casting. Then, once cast, discuss and study each character with those chosen to play it.

I once saw a production of *Mindgame* by Anthony Horowitz where the character of the wife was played by a woman who was totally wooden and quite awful. She had obviously not understood the situation and why she was saying what she was saying. All she did was recite the lines on the page with about as much enthusiasm and understanding as a racing snail.

Who you are, you discover by a close and careful study of the lines you are to speak, the body language and physical reaction of the person you are saying them to, and also to some extent by the lines that are delivered back to you. They may indicate whether your character is loved or hated.

Develop your character. Put yourself into your character's head. Research everything you can on the character's possible life, especially if they live in a different time period. Come up with all the little details you can. Put yourself into their life. You can become the character by writing down their characteristics and voice projection. If they're really shy, you could write down, "Shy: Look at feet, bite your lip, play with objects as if nervous." Emotion is what makes an actor, so really understand what you are saying. If you know your character well enough, you will also understand their emotions. Use emphasis on important words to get your point across. Be dramatic.

So many productions fail because this process is not carried out.

The role you are playing can also be made better – or worse – by facial expressions. The classic example of this I think is Rowan Atkinson playing Mr. Bean or Blackadder. His use of facial expressions adds so much to the character even when there is no dialogue.

Sometimes you may be in a scene with a couple of others and have a few moments without saying any lines. You must try to stay in character and react to what is being said by using facial expressions and body language. For example, hands in pockets might say relaxed or bored, but folded arms suggest you are being defensive, and regularly looking at your watch could suggest impatience if that is what is required

So important is characterisation that many directors begin working on it as soon as the plan of production is blocked out.

KEY POINTS

Analyse the text thoroughly
Find out who your character really is
Study and use body language

What Do I Want

Another way of asking this might be to ask yourself where does my role lead me. Where will I be at the end of the story? Am I a hero or villain? Do I get the girl or rob the bank?

The answers to these questions lie, no not in the soil, but in the author's words on the page. So we come back to text analysis.

Take a look at the following extract from The Mechanicals scene in Shakespeare's *A Midsummer Night's Dream*.

QUINCE
Answer as I call you. Nick Bottom, the weaver.

BOTTOM
Ready. Name what part I am for, and proceed.

QUINCE
You, Nick Bottom, are set down for Pyramus.

BOTTOM
*What is Pyramus? a lover, or a **tyrant**?*

QUINCE
A lover, that kills himself most gallant for love.

BOTTOM
That will ask some tears in the true performing of it. If I do it, let the audience look to their eyes; I will move storms, I will condole in some measure. To the rest yet my chief humour is for a tyrant: I could play Ercles rarely, or a part to tear a cat in, to make all split.

The raging rocks
And shivering shocks

Shall break the locks
Of prison gates;
And Phibbus' car
Shall shine from far
And make and mar
The foolish Fates.
This was lofty! Now name the rest of the players. This is Ercles' vein, a tyrant's vein; a lover is more condoling.

QUINCE

Francis Flute, the bellows-mender.

FLUTE

Here, Peter Quince.

QUINCE

Flute, you must take Thisbe on you.

FLUTE

What is Thisbe? a wandering knight?

QUINCE

It is the lady that Pyramus must love.

FLUTE

*Nay, faith, let me not play a woman; **I have a beard** coming.*

QUINCE

That's all one: you shall play it in a mask, and you may speak as small as you will.

BOTTOM

And I may hide my face, let me play Thisbe too, I'll speak in a monstrous little voice. 'Thisne, Thisne; – 'Ah, Pyramus, lover dear! thy Thisbe dear, and lady dear!'

QUINCE

No, no; you must play Pyramus: and, Flute, you Thisbe.

BOTTOM
Well, proceed.

QUINCE
Robin Starveling, the tailor.

STARVELING
Here, Peter Quince.

QUINCE
Robin Starveling, you must play Thisbe's mother. Tom Snout, the tinker.

SNOUT
Here, Peter Quince.

QUINCE
You, Pyramus' father, myself, Thisby's father, Snug, the joiner, you, the lion's part: and I hope here is a play fitted.

SNUG
Have you the lion's part written? pray you, if it be, give it me for I am slow of study.

QUINCE
You may do it extempore, for it is nothing but roaring.

BOTTOM
Let me play the lion too **I will roar,** *that I will do any man's heart good to hear me. I will roar, that I will make the Duke say 'Let him roar again,* **let him roar again'**

QUINCE
And you should do it too terribly, you would fright the Duchess and the ladies, that **they would shriek;** *and that were enough to hang us all.*

ALL
That would hang us, every mother's son.

BOTTOM
I grant you, friends, if that you should fright the ladies out of their wits, they would have no more discretion but to hang us. But I will aggravate my voice so that I will roar you as gently as any sucking dove; **I will roar you an 'twere any nightingale.**

QUINCE
You can play no part but Pyramus; *for Pyramus is a sweet-faced man; a proper man as one shall see in a summer's day; a most lovely gentleman-like man: therefore you must needs play Pyramus.*

BOTTOM
Well, I will undertake it. What beard were I best to play it in?

Consider the characters Quince and Bottom and look at the words I have highlighted.

Quince is clearly in charge but Bottom thinks he can play all the parts.

Now add a couple of accents. Remember the Mechanicals are just that and not "gentry", so a strong regional accent for all of them will help bring out their characters.

Many think Shakespeare is difficult, but as you can see from this short extract it is pretty straightforward – once you analyse the text.

Check your lines in the play you are going to be in and look for the keywords and "use" them as in the above example and your character will be the better for it.

KEY POINTS

Look "inside" the text
Think about your speech style
Find the keywords

How Do I Get There

Do we always mean what we say? I doubt it. The same applies with some lines for characters. However, there are often clues as to the direction and scheme an author has chosen for his characters which move the plot forward.

Be the character. "Drama" means "To do". You are not merely *pretending* to be someone else; here, you are *actually being* someone else!

Think for a moment about the character you are playing and ask yourself, "If I was him would I really say or do this, and if so why?"

Take this a stage further in relation to the dialogue that is coming back to you and you will really begin to get inside your role.

So you can now see I hope that a great deal depends on a thorough knowledge and understanding of the script.

Putting make-up on your face and uttering words of three syllables or more does not make you an actor.

Look again at the example above from The Mechanicals and try reading one of the characters aloud without any pauses or inflection – read it like a shopping list. Sounds dreadful, right?

Now read it again, but this time add pauses where there is punctuation, look at what is being said and why.

Try emphasising the words I have highlighted and hear the difference. Better still record it on to a disc or cassette and listen to it back.

How different is it now?

This is how we begin to analyse text and now we discover that the piece is beginning to come alive.

Another key factor is appearance, or dress. If your character is an up-market businessman or similar, it is unlikely he would have scruffy clothes or dirty shoes. As in everyday life, how people present themselves very often tells you the sort of person they really are.

Think also about body language. When we communicate with each other, the impact of what is being said hits us from three sources. Body language accounts for 55%, the voice quality for 38% and the voice for 7%. Think about this when you see, watch or meet people. It is very often the non-verbal cues that the listener will pay attention to.

KEY POINTS

Get inside the script
Read it out loud
Visualise the character and action "for real"
Emphasise body language

The Voice

Okay, so you have memorised your words, but what do they mean and how do they sound?

Your use of pauses, inflection, emphasis, possible accents, and whether you drop your "aitches" or not will all be part of creating your role.

Enunciate. This means you have to say your words the way they are meant to be said. Of course, you shouldn't do that if it isn't what your character would do. But almost all the time, you will be required to enunciate. Don't you hate it when you're listening to someone speaking or maybe listening to a song and all of a sudden you hear a jumble of noises. You get frustrated because you don't know what in the world was just said. Enunciate to avoid this happening to your audience.

Listen to your favourite comedian or words from a great dramatic actor in a strong scene and consider what they say – the actual words they use. If you repeated their actual words in a normal conversational voice often it would not seem very funny or dramatic. So how do they do it?

Simple – they use pauses, emphasis, yes that's emphasis, pitch, tone, volume and pace of delivery. End result: it becomes strongly dramatic or very funny.

Take for example the following quotation from Shakespeare's *Hamlet*, Perhaps one of the best known quotations from the Bard.

> *"To be or Not to be*
> *That is the question."*

Say it without any "use" of your voice. Now try it this way:

> *"To BE (pause) or not to BE (pause)*
> *THAT is the question"*

Try this a few times – now you can see what I am getting at. Now try the same thing with lines from the script you are working on. Play around with the words and phrases in your lines and you will be surprised how varied they can be. Plus it helps you get inside the role you are playing and also you start to remember your lines.

With time and imaginative consideration a vast difference can be made.

How often have you seen a play and found the characters simply unbelievable. The voice, manner, dress, deportment and so on, just nothing connects or gets even near to the character you are supposed to be following

Think on this for a moment. Imagine that this is the first time you have ever said the line and then extend that feeling and apply the same thought to the lines that are delivered to you. So effectively each time you say your lines or respond to those coming at you, your reaction will be fresh and therefore more "alive".

Many scripts tell us, "man, 25ish, businesslike" for instance. Others do not, so we have to gather clues from the text.

What for example does the following extract from my monologue "A Few Words" tell us about the speaker.

Dear friends how many times have you heard in a few words – some profound thought or greeting simply put in just a few words.

Dear friends simple they may be but were they enough. Indeed have you ever asked yourself the simple question – in a few words – am I getting enough.

Dear friends even in these few words – ARE YOU GETTING ENOUGH – there is a feeling of simple yet profound language. Even here – there may be a sense of extra or spare words and so my dear friends you might need to ask yourself if you have actually come across a bit of spare.

(look hard at someone in the front row)
Perhaps – in a few words – I can give another example in a few words.

You can reasonably assume the text suggests that the character is a vicar but perhaps with a humorous or even perverted side to his character. Read between the lines and you can see how he connects with the audience with suggestive words and by looking hard at someone in the front row.

Amateur productions do not use mics, so it is essential that those in the play project their voices.

You have to "feel" the part, because a sweet voice on its own is simply not enough.

How often have you watched a production and been unable to hear some of the lines simply because the person in that role did not project their voice.

By projection I do not mean shouting. Simply speak clearly and imagine that in the back row there is someone who is slightly deaf, so speak up so they can hear you.

Don't swallow your words. Don't speak too fast. What you're saying can be lost no matter how loud you are talking.

When directing I always stand at the back of the hall so I can judge projection and get the actor or actress to speak up so I can hear them.

KEY POINTS

Use pauses and emphasise key words
Get inside the script
Learn to project
Do not mutter

Improvisation

The benefits of improvisation exercises – or games – can be significant in many ways.

They can, and do, build confidence in being in front of a group or audience. They get people thinking on their feet and can definitely be a lot of fun.

There are many physical and speech routines that can be used and here are two improvisation games to try out.

The first requires your group to work in pairs.

Pair number one split, with one of them leaving the room for a couple of minutes. In their absence the other one invents and creates a character. The first person then returns to the scene and through questioning – perhaps playing the role of a detective – tries to identify the other character.

This can be both creative and confidence building.

The second "game" is one I often used when tutoring courses on communication skills, including public speaking.

I get everyone to write down on a piece of paper a topic for someone else to give a talk on. The point is the topic has to be ridiculous. For example, "A day in the life of a tramp's sock" or "Life inside a ping-pong ball".

All notes are put in a hat, then each person picks one out. They have three minutes to think about it, then three minutes to speak on it.

It is a lot of fun but also very useful. The point is if you can stand in front of a group of people and talk on a weird topic without prep time for three minutes, think what you can do with a script, time to learn it and a good director.

KEY POINTS

Improvisation "games" help create characters and increase confidence.

Learning Your Lines

The ways people learn lines are many and varied. It's not really justified to say any particular method is best. Each to his own.

Those of us old enough to have learnt the times tables at school by rote still remember them – instantly.

That is how I learn my lines – by rote.

My method is simple and usually its bedtime reading.

When you get your own copy of the script, highlight or underline your lines. Cover the page except for your first line or sentence. Read it several times out loud. Cover it again and repeat it and see how much you can remember. Repeat this until that first line is in the memory. Then move down to the next. Repeat the process, read and memorise, then read and run the two lines together. Follow this pattern down the page, then the first thing the next morning do it again and you should find it has gone in.

It is essential that you say it out loud. You may think that you can learn by reading it to yourself, but it is not so effective.

Like anything else, you do best what you have practiced, so make sure you go through your lines in the way you need to say them. Project them clearly, with emphasis in the right way, and of course emotion and any accent that is required. Just knowing the words isn't enough.

In addition, by reading it aloud you begin to get the flow of the dialogue.

So when do you start learning?

As soon as you get your copy of the script.

Another useful method is as soon as the script has been chosen for all the cast to read it out loud and for it to be recorded so when you are at home or in the car you can play it over and over again. It really does work.

Personally I am never happy until someone can give me random cues, from anywhere in the script, and I can come back with my line correctly. When I can do that I am confident, and apart from anything else it is a tremendous antidote to stage fright.

I aim for this point at least two weeks prior to production, but having reached the comfort zone I still go through my part each day just to keep it fresh.

Anything can happen when a live performance is involved. And those errors include forgotten lines. Whether the actors are simply rattled by something personal or their memories briefly "turn off", the end result is the same: a mistake where lines disappear into the ether and everyone on stage is stumped… if not panicked… at least for a few seconds.

If you find yourself in this circumstance, though, you needn't lose control. Relax, breathe, and just start talking "in character". Often, when you begin speaking, you can get yourself back on track and pick up where you left off in your acting.

Should you be working with an actor who forgets his or her lines, you can always help by jumping in to advance the dialogue in a natural manner to cover the mistake. If you don't show your anxiety, the audience will likely never realise what happened.

However the bottom line is, really learning your lines will give you confidence and help you put more into the role you are playing.

KEY POINTS

Begin learning your lines as soon as you get the script
Aim for total lines at least two weeks ahead of first night

Production Publicity

Okay, so the play is chosen and cast, the stage crew are making their plans, and the village hall is booked and paid for. Now what?

As rehearsals start, so should publicity.

After all, you need bums on seats to cover all expenses. So where do you start?

Your group will probably set up a website, so an awful of information can go on there. Not just the play and performance date but maybe some personal details of the cast – with their permission of course – their previous experience and so forth.

Information can often be placed in the local paper and the local radio station who will certainly have an events slot.

Then of course there are flyers or posters to go up around the area. It is also a good idea to send information to other groups within say a ten mile radius. This works both ways with mutual support.

One thing is certain. You cannot get too much publicity.

As far as posters are concerned, how about this. Put photos of a couple of the cast on them, then when the posters are in local shop windows the cast will be recognised by some locals in addition to friends. This may well help to bring in more audience members.

KEY POINTS

Publicity matters
Leave no stone unturned
Include other groups in you campaign

Directing

If the director honestly wants to direct, if he really wants to put on a clear, intelligent, dramatic production, he should accept the responsibility for ensuring the performance is well acted.

The director needs to bring the actors together, explain the play and characters, then sit back and observe, guiding where necessary.

After all, his purpose is to present a play in a way which will give his audience the greatest experience possible, and the actors become material to be used in the creation of a well-acted play.

The first thing the director often needs to do is to explain the difference between exhibitionism and acting.

Many actors are stimulated through their feelings. Of course, they need to have an adequate conception of the character in mind; but the mental conception does not stimulate them to imitation. They haven't reasoned very much about the character, but they have felt about him. And they must be made to feel more; they must be impressed before they will be able to act.

The director, in the case of this person, takes the position of the impressive orator. He stops the scene. He builds up atmosphere, for instance a tragic scene where we picture the feelings of the young mother as she weeps over the death of her first born; and the actress, wide-eyed, drinks in the story in silence for she, in that moment, has changed places with the imaginary mother. Then quietly the director says: "Now let's try the scene again." He says nothing more for a while. Under the spell of the emotion, he will allow the actress to speak the lines of the mother; and the feeling engendered in the actress impels her into the character.

Because she feels sincerely, her voice and actions are in harmony with the character. The characterisation may not be perfect, and she may lose some of it at a subsequent rehearsal;

but she has made a start; a door into the character has been opened and the actress will perhaps know how to open it again.

In scenes perhaps as emotional as this example, the director should give thought, time and encouragement to the person playing such a character.

Nothing happens to the actor for a time, because he is busy building up his idea of the character. It should go without saying that the director has to know the answers to the questions asked and the answers to some questions the actor doesn't think to ask. He must be able to explain the character, his exact position in the scheme of the play, the motivation for this or that action, the reason for such and such a speech. Then, after much time has been spent on this exposition, the actor begins to reveal the character in his acting.

Whoever is directing should also permit the actor a certain creative opportunity and freedom of expression but should always remain the director, after all he has something which he wishes to have expressed, but the actor is the one who must actually give expression to it. Therefore the director says: "Here is what I wish done in this scene. Here is the mood you shall have; here is the emotion. Now go ahead."

The actor takes the plan as outlined. He can create, but only within the limitations set. He can use his own inflections and pauses and can express the mood and emotion according to his own ideas; but if these ideas are at variance with the director's plan, they must be discarded, or at least talked through with the director.

Sometimes it may be necessary to place the actor completely under the will of the director who, instead of permitting the actor freedom, prescribes that he shall do exactly as told and nothing more.

The actor becomes the material with which the director works, just as the script becomes the material with which the actor works.

Above all, the director should get the cast to portray their characters in a way that makes the play work and brings out the story in depth.

Unfortunately this does not always happen,

I recently saw a production of *Last Tango in Little Grimley* by David Tristram – one of a number of very funny pieces about Amateur Theatre.

The director clearly had not studied the script or "created" the characters, especially that of the "Director" in the story. Result – the character was wooden and had no humour apart from the words on the page. A great pity because so much more could have been achieved.

So when you are directing think about the character and what sort of person he or she would really be like and bring it out of your actors.

If any cast members are not feeling comfortable get them to try different improvisation exercises to get them focused and put the rhythm of the play back on track.

So important is characterisation that many directors begin working on it as soon as the plan of production is blocked out.

"Blocking" refers to the directions you give to the actors about where to go on the stage, when, and how. If you have a show with a lot of quick changes, blocking ahead of time is a MUST. Give your actors directions and make sure they write them down. You don't want to waste time arguing about whether you told them to cross upstage or downstage. I would recommend to anyone directing a production to begin blocking after the first read-through.

It will also help the cast to memorise the lines by linking them to a particular move.

Good scenery does not excuse bad acting, and because many directors do not have the passion or experience, they sometimes think that good scenery makes a good production. It does not work like that. The production essentially depends on the cast, director and, of course, a good script. So, as I said, the director must bring the actors together, explain the play and characters, and what he hopes to achieve in each scene.

Discuss the mood and the emotion the cast must have. They must then take the plan as outlined and create, but only within the limitations set. They must use their own inflections, pauses and body language to express the mood and emotion according to the ideas outlined.

The baseline to sum it up is to bring in your emotions because you only start acting when you stop trying to act. However this does not mean that the director is redundant. Far from it.

This approach will keep a unity of production and, at the same time, give the cast a share in the creation of the play.

The director needs to encourage the cast to learn their lines totally not later than two weeks before the first night. And, as the work proceeds, he can keep his eyes open to see that his demands are not too great. He has much to do, but he should be considerate of what his actors are asked to do. They cannot create a part in a few days. They cannot remember every little detail he tells them. They cannot work until midnight and be fresh and clear-minded at the next rehearsal.

Both the director and the cast have a great deal to accomplish before the play is ready for an audience, and a very limited amount of time in which to accomplish it, so the director must concentrate on the work at hand, unbroken by interruptions, otherwise valuable time will be wasted. He must have discipline from the first meeting of the cast.

The actors must know that rehearsal time is for attentive work on the play, that rehearsals begin at the hour scheduled, that they proceed as any serious job should proceed, that people are to be ready to take their entrances without being called, and that it is the business of the actors, as well as the director, to follow the scene being played. Such discipline of the rehearsal period is essential, whether the actors are mature men and women or youngsters.

After all, the work of production must be finished by a set date.

KEY POINTS

Work on emotion of the part
Do not confuse good scenery with good production
Concentrate and focus on the character

Rehearsals Start

This is the birthplace of the production.

The director should take charge from the beginning emphasising time and also quiet, so don't forget to turn off all mobiles. People cannot concentrate and rehearse properly if others are chatting in the corner, it does not work.

Often directors are to blame. I have seen them happily chatting to someone whilst the cast are trying to work. Gross bad form by the director who should give 100% concentration to the cast.

I believe this also rules out following the book as a substitute for watching the cast. If you are reading the text as it is being delivered you cannot watch what is going on. That is another reason and benefit of the director having a thorough knowledge of the script before rehearsals start.

Up to now it has only been words on the page.

The majority of groups rehearse on average two nights a week for maybe eight weeks, with perhaps an increase in the last couple of weeks before production. However, pantomimes and musicals do generally take longer, although there are no hard and fast rules. I have known some to work on a production for four months, one night per week. This I would hate and feel it would ensure that everyone was fed up to the back teeth with it by the time of production. A shorter intensive schedule gets my vote but it does depend on several factors, including the availability of rehearsal space and also the length of the play. Obviously a one-act play takes less time than one with three or four acts.

When planning your schedule – unless it is only one act, don't expect to do the whole play every time, apart that is from the first couple of meetings. If you do you will get nowhere.

Full run-throughs should be aimed for towards the end of the rehearsal schedule, so for example in a nine-week plan aim for a run-through at about six weeks and in the meantime break the play down at least into acts or scenes and not necessarily in the running order.

It is natural to logically give roughly equal time to each act or scene but sometimes a specific section needs more concentration, so on occasions you may need to work on shorter sections. These may be only a couple of pages but may contain a seismic shift in the storyline.

This may also give some people a night off if they are not needed.

If the director has done sufficient preparation this should already be in the diary.

After a few rehearsals you should become aware of the areas which are weaker, thus allowing a schedule change.

The basics are obvious, like anything else in life that has to be learned, the more you do it the better it gets. However rehearsals are not just about learning your lines, they are about action and reaction.

They are not about you and your friends but about the relationship of the characters you are playing.

Rehearsals must be fun but at the same time they must be disciplined. After all, in just a few weeks you will be up on stage in front of a paying audience.

If for any reason you need to leave the stage area between exits and entrances, first make sure you have time to do what you need to do! Nothing slows up a rehearsal and breaks the flow of the action onstage like the words "Oh, he's in the loo" or "Damn, has she gone outside for a smoke?"

It also helps to let the stage manager or another person backstage know where you're going.

Do your best, have fun, and don't let anyone bring you down. A big part of acting is being prepared for criticism, or perhaps even heckling. Remain positive and work hard to be successful.

Whilst generally the set will not be ready for the early rehearsals it is worthwhile using props from a very early stage, wherever possible. Not only do you get used to them, but it helps in building a scene – even if it is only a tray of tea or a telephone. This will also help with learning lines that are linked to a specific action or prop movement.

If your character is not in a scene or perhaps is "absent" from say Act two, it is useful to watch the rehearsal of the other sections. This will help you get "inside" the story – indeed there may be references to your role by the other characters. All these points will help you "identify" who you are.

KEY POINTS

Director must concentrate
Do not cause disruption
Start on time
Use small props from the start

Starting To Move

Now an important factor is where you rehearse. You may be very lucky and work on the stage where your production will take place. However, it is more likely that it will be a room in a pub, somebody's front room or even the garage.

The point is you need reasonable space to create your "stage", perhaps using chairs and tables that you would actually require on stage. You also need to identify doors where your actors will enter and exit.

Your script may well give directions such as;

(John enters upstage and stands by mirror).

An experienced director may well ignore this if the move is not vital to the plot and put an alternative move in, but if you are starting from scratch these directions will be a great help to you.

Moves also help the cast remember lines.

One common mistake is that of "masking", of one actor standing behind another. This is bad practice if for no other reason than the audience cannot see them, and so should be avoided, except where it is essential to the story. If actors find themselves masked by someone "downstage" (that is nearer the audience) they should adjust their position to one side or the other.

Never turn your back to the audience, unless there is a reason and it has been plotted by the director.

You and your fellow cast members may know the script, but the audience does not, so, if you mumble a line, especially when facing away from the audience, they won't be able to hear you and won't know what's going on.

Stay aware of your position. When performing in a play, you should somewhat talk to the audience as you talk to fellow actors during the play. This is particularly relevant in a pantomime of course

Sometimes you might think that it is necessary to talk louder or project, so when rehearsing get somebody to stand as far away from the stage as possible and see if he or she can hear you. Logically this is likely to be the director.

You have to be audible. Also, don't swallow your words and don't speak too fast. What you're saying can be lost no matter how loud you are talking.

Keep the play flowing. Imagine a person wasting seconds to get to their place on stage. Do that a lot and the audience will lose interest, so be aware.

When I am directing, unless reasons for moves are specific and compelling, I concentrate on the dialogue and interaction between the characters. This often creates "natural" moves which will happen once the actors are well inside the character. However there may be a direction in the script which says, for example, "John moves to rear window as she screams". In this situation specific moves may be required.

When on stage it is not just the spoken word that counts but body language and facial expressions.

Next time you are in a bar or restaurant, quietly look and watch others and you will see what I mean. We can say a lot without actually speaking out loud so learn to react to others even if you have no dialogue at that moment. Sometimes during dialogue people will move naturally and that is fine providing it does not compromise the storyline.

KEY POINTS

Do not be masked
Identify with your role
Always consider the audience when you move and position yourself on stage
Moves must appear normal unless initiated by dialogue

Stage Manager

If the director "controls" the cast, the stage manager "controls" the set.

The job is essential and he or she should be involved as soon as the play has been chosen and rehearsals start.

The role in essence involves organising the set and scenery, together with props and perhaps special effects. It is also a good idea to have an assistant stage manager as two pairs of hands are always better than one.

In any script there will be directions about effects, lighting, set changes and props.

If there are several set changes or many requirements for prop movement, it is a good idea to decide who moves what – and stick to it. That way you will avoid confusion and the possibility of the wrong thing ending up in the wrong place.

The stage manager and any member of the stage crew will need a copy of the script as soon as it is chosen and cast so they can mark up their jobs.

At the end of each performance it is the job of the stage crew to reset ready for the following opening.

Where furniture or props or parts of the set have not been moved there may be little to do. It is, though, essential that the SM does a check to make sure everything is in place.

KEY POINTS

Plan all moves and stick to them
Check set before each performance

The Set

Having chosen the play, early discussions are needed with your stage manager and artistic designer if you have one to decide on the design and appearance of the set.

In general terms, it is my belief that the simpler the set the better. I would put forward the case that if the script is good and it is well directed and performed, the set can sometimes be almost irrelevant. The one major exception to that line of thought is of course a pantomime.

Whilst many contemporary, and indeed some classical plays are staged with little or no set, most amateur productions work in a set. The design and appearance, whilst the province of the director, needs the skills of carpenters, artists and painters, at the very least.

Every play needs a different set and although the "flats" – sections of scenery that are the "walls" – are repeatedly used they will almost always have to be repainted.

So we have our flats to create say a living room which is illuminated, but how about the furniture and "props", a bookcase for instance with books to fill it. A variety of items that would normally appear in a living room have to be acquired, suitable of course to the period in which the play is set. Essentially do not clutter the stage with anything that is not needed as a prop or to create the mood or style.

Here somebody will take on the job as "props" and it will be their responsibility to beg, borrow or, if absolutely necessary, purchase the required items. Charity shops can be a very good source at low cost.

One thing which should be obvious is to make sure that a picture or anything attached on the wall or "flat" is actually fixed. Nothing creates a laugh or is more embarrassing than part of the scenery falling down for no apparent reason.

A set, of course, is no good without the actors who may need costumes, wigs, make-up etc, again depending upon the date of the action.

Again these can often be obtained from charity shops or hired from costume specialists. However, if the play is modern it is probably not necessary to hire or buy.

KEY POINTS

Keep it simple
Don't clutter the stage
Make sure fixtures are fixed

Effects

Some plays and probably many pantomimes have a certain point in the story where a flash pot or smoke effect is required.

Smoke and pyrotechnic effects must be used with care. All the equipment should have clear operating instructions. There are many different types of "smoke machines" available, and many rely on converting a liquid into a mist using heat and a catalyst so a typical smoke machine can produce a fine haze or a pea-souper fog.

Another effect is known as dry ice. Made with frozen carbon dioxide, it is dropped into warm water resulting in condensation and the formation of fog. It will stay low because it is cooler than the surrounding air and is non-toxic and, also, as the fog mixes with the surrounding air, it quickly warms and evaporates.

Ice and smoke effects can help create magical scenes but problems may arise in small village halls and the like as such effects are likely to set off the smoke detectors and fire alarm which will disrupt the show.

To create instant effects like flashes of light and puffs of smoke pyrotechnic charges can be used. Nowadays these have been refined to make them as safe as possible and easy to use. The charge is contained in a small pod that plugs into a special holder. The charge is fired by a low voltage remote control, with a key switch to avoid accidental operation.

These effects can be obtained and are easy to set up and fire. However, there is a golden rule that is whoever sets it off must have direct line of sight to the device in order to avoid accidents.

KEY POINTS

Operator must have line of sight to "firing" point
Use all smoke and pyrotechnic equipment with care

Stage Sound and Music

Sound is often left to the last minute, probably because of the inconvenience of setting up the equipment, as it often has to be packed away between rehearsals. The simplest set-up will require a CD or tape player, some form of amplification and speakers.

In the past a good quality home cassette tape machine did the job, or a reel-to-reel tape recorder which gave a better quality playback and made it easy to cue the tape to the start of a recording. Alternatively you could record your music and effects on to a compact disc. A home hi-fi amplifier and speakers might be powerful enough for incidental music at a smaller venue, but using the amplifier at full output may distort the sound and could do permanent damage to the amplifier and speakers.

For best results get a professional power amplifier, but remember your cast will be distracted if the effects are too loud for them to work.

Even if the stage directions do not indicate that a particular piece of music should be played before the play or during the interval, think about what might create the right atmosphere. For example if the play you are doing is staged in the 1930s, a big band piece of music will help create the right atmosphere setting the scene and also the mood for the audience.

Also if you play a specific piece of music just before the curtains open at the start of the play, when the audience hear the same music later during the interval they will realise that it signifies the next part of the show.

Almost every production will involve some sound effects. Just how you achieve the result you want will depend on how many effects you need and what they are. Many recorded effects are commercially available or can be downloaded free from various websites, although the quality of some effects may not be clear enough for theatre use.

In pantomime, music is essential with usually a number of songs or dances in the script.

If you can, get someone who plays a keyboard to do the music live rather than have it recorded. The result is usually much better.

KEY POINTS .

Get sound system balanced
If possible use "live" music

Prompt Copy

This is something quite specific. It is not just another copy of the script but an important tool for whoever will be prompt. Once rehearsals start it is essential that whoever the prompt is, they attend all sessions. In that way they will understand where the pauses come in the action and dialogue, as well as any changes to the words. Otherwise one of the characters may get a prompt where a dramatic pause is required as part of the action. If no prompt was required it would ruin the scene.

If you are prompt, make a note of pauses and so forth in your copy. It may also be your job, perhaps, to ring a bell at a certain moment. Again highlight this in the script.

So is a prompt necessary?

It is a safety net, but I do remember a pantomime we did where the director stated right from the start that there would be no prompt. Result! Everybody learnt their lines very thoroughly. His statement instilled discipline which paid off.

However, the opposite was true in a local play festival I watched. In one of the entries a female cast member had not learnt her lines – big time. So bad was she that she kept edging towards prompt corner and making gestures that she needed a prompt. This happened throughout that particular 30 minute play. It was a disaster.

KEY POINTS

Attend every rehearsal
Highlight pauses

Run-through

Once rehearsals have been well under way for perhaps three of four weeks with different nights for various sections, it will be time to consider doing a full run-through.

There comes a point where you need to see the whole thing. Ok, it is not yet ready for performance but it is coming together and everyone needs to see it in its entirety, plus it will help the director spot any weak points that will need extra work.

Doing run-throughs helps knit the play together and gives everybody greater confidence in the whole project. Plus it enables you to get a fairly accurate idea of the time frame.

Try to get in as many run-throughs as possible before the dress rehearsal, ironing out glitches as you go. You may be surprised as to how good it looks and it also gives the cast a feeling of something achieved.

These rehearsals are undoubtedly for your actors' benefit but are also important for your production crew.

Stage, sound and lighting crew – techies – all work behind the scenes and this is their only time with all the pieces together to work out the kinks. Value your crews, because they are equal in importance to the cast on the stage.

Lighting cues require timing, as do sound cues. Allow your techies to be involved in the notes sessions so they can work out their issues and ask questions. Tech run is a final rehearsal just for techies. Please schedule one.

KEY POINTS

Start run-throughs ASAP
Everybody must be involved

Make-up

Make-up is used to complement actors' facial characteristics or to disguise them. It also needs to work with their costume and stage character and compensate for the effect of the stage lighting on their complexion. Also consider the location of the story. If in the tropics for example there would be suntan, or in Victorian London something to clarify poverty and dirt.

When applying your make-up make sure you have a clear work surface in the dressing room with a mirror and good lighting.

Close up your make-up may seem a little primitive, but you have to allow for the fact that most of the audience are quite a distance from the stage. Always check the make-up under the actual stage lighting, this is best done at dress rehearsal with someone sitting in the audience to check for you.

Simple make-up will consist of a base of either a pancake (water-based or powder), cream or grease stick make-up about one shade deeper than the natural skin tone. Grease sticks are a heavier make-up than cream and are known by the Leichner numbers; number five (Ivory) and number nine (Brick Red) are popular numbers for men. Peach rouge is popular for women. Avoid red, as it is most unnatural, unless that is the type of effect you want to create!

Certainly in pantomimes make-up is essential, but in straight plays – especially modern ones – it is not used a great deal unless a character needs a "scar" or some other defining mark.

You may need to disguise or add to the actors' appearance and a typical way to do this is to use a beard or moustache for men and wigs or hairpieces for either sex. Experienced make-up artists will use crêpe hair. Ready-made hairpieces are easier, but not always as realistic.

In my opinion, apart from pantomimes it is better to use as little make-up as possible.

KEY POINTS

Check appearance under stage lighting from audience area
Use only when really necessary

Technical Rehearsal

In a pantomime where there may be a great many lighting changes, sound effects, smoke effects or flashpots being used in addition to music, a tech rehearsal is an absolute necessity.

Basically go through all cues for changes and effects to ensure continuity.

Of course, in a straight play it may not be necessary, as changes will no doubt be minimal. However double-checking and "testing" everything will add to the smooth running of the performances.

Dress Rehearsal

This is the final run-through before opening night. Run the play like a full performance with no stops other than the planned interval. Certainly there should be no interruptions from the director. Any comments should be kept until the performance has been completed. Any glitches can then be discussed, although by now it is too late for significant changes.

This may seem a little strange but in my experience a perfect dress rehearsal sometimes leads to a first night that is less than perfect. Perhaps it creates too much confidence.

Certainly when we had the odd minor problem during the dress, the first night went much better, so perhaps it helps everybody to concentrate that little bit more.

Another thing that sometimes gets overlooked is the watch and the wedding ring. If you are married but the character you are playing is not, remember to remove your ring. Equally the opposite may apply.

Little details like this can make a difference between an average show and a really good show.

The old saying, "Look after the pennies and the pounds will look after themselves" is true in many aspects of life and certainly relevant in theatre

Attention to detail matters. Certainly everybody needs to be at the dress rehearsal and this definitely includes the front of house crew. They need to be sure of when the main house lights go on and off.

KEY POINTS

Check all small details

Front of House

The meet and greet crew, or Front of House, are also an essential part of the team. This crew will be running the box office and also may arrange seating in the hall including space for wheelchairs. They may also be organising refreshments in the interval.

Another job for FOH may well be running a raffle with prizes, hopefully donated. This is another way of raising money for the group.

In addition, part of their duty will probably be the switching on and off of house lights.

It may seem obvious, but not long ago I went to see a one-act play festival, where at the end of the interval the main hall lights were left on for no reason. It was bad for the audience and very distracting for the cast. There was obviously no co-ordination or communication between FOH and the stage crew, which if you think about it is a basic essential towards the smooth running of a show.

One way of making this easy is to have a simple radio system so SM and FOH can communicate easily

Another duty of the FOH crew may be making announcements. For example just before the performance starts, "Good evening and welcome to tonight's performance. Please make sure all mobile phones are switched off." Other topics may also be required such as smoking not allowed, location of fire exits and where to assemble in the event of an evacuation.

When selling tickets for your events, you'll need someone to manage seating arrangements, tickets, complementary tickets for the local press and similar matters.

Though the box office manager's role has sometimes been seen as not very important, it is an indicator of the society's attitude and professionalism. By appointing a FOH manager who is sensible, straightforward, and thorough, your group will ensure that no one arrives on opening night only to find out their seats have been sold!

Tickets and programmes of course are a cost to the production but are necessary. The programme can often pay for itself if you can get local businesses to support the production by placing an advert in it.

In addition to the cast and information about the play, why not put some biographical details in about those included.

KEY POINTS

Have effective co-ordination and communication with backstage
Forward planning is essential

First Night

So the hard work is done and now for the fun. If you have learnt your lines "backwards" and everything else is in place, "stage fright" should be cut by 90%.

Yes it is still there a little, but this keeps you on your toes.

Most performers have experienced stage fright at one time or another. Most of the time people can't help being a little nervous, and that's fine! The trick is to control it.

Having too much stress before you go out on stage will compromise your performance. A little bit of nervous energy is good and can fuel your performance, but too much will hurt it. Not to mention damage to your confidence for future performances.

The core problem for many people is a lack of confidence. Confidence is the answer to overcoming stage fright and having good stage presence. It's having confidence that will allow you the freedom to dance around and enjoy your experience on the stage, and because of that your stage presence will come out naturally!

Overactive nerves and the fear that your audience will not like you causes stage fright. Treat "nerves" as excitement and you will feel the difference.

If there is time, do a rapid word run through the whole play with the cast. No movement, no props, just a rapid gabble as fast as you can. This acts as a warm-up but also reassures you.

Relax. Take a deep breath. It helps a lot of people if they tense up their entire body and keep it that way for a few seconds. Then, just relax all your muscles. "Box breathing" is also a good method. Breathe in for four seconds, hold for four seconds, breathe out for four seconds. The overall effect is very relaxing.

Another thing to mention that's extremely important is not to take yourself too seriously. Do not be afraid to laugh at yourself if you make a mistake. It is not the end of the world and by having the ability to lighten up you will be better for it.

Having good stage presence stems firstly from confidence on stage. It will help get rid of stage fright and help enjoy performing and gaining stage presence.

Be sure that when it's your time to go on stage or enter the scene, you're ready to go, meaning that you are in character, you have your props, and you know your lines. Listen for your cue. Don't get distracted by chatting to the crew in the wings.

It is useful to get into the habit of checking your script as soon as you get offstage to see when you're up next and where you need to be. However after doing this thoroughly in rehearsals, you should not need to check any more – you should automatically know where to be and how much time you have to get there.

Remember that it's not all about you – the production is a team effort, something that requires all the people involved. The person with the least number of words is as important as the leading role.

Do your part, be supportive of the group, and work together to make the show the best it can be because that is what really matters.

Release your inhibitions.

That does not mean having an alcoholic drink before you go on. Many of us like a glass (or three) but leave it until after the performance has finished. I certainly like a drink, but never ever before the show. Over the years I have seen real mess-ups as a result of someone drinking before the performance.

Acting is much easier if you aren't constantly worrying about how others will perceive you. Remember that audience members won't see you doing whatever you're doing, they see what your character is doing.

Always believe that you can do it. This belief alone will often carry you through a mishap and bring your audience with you. It will also make you feel more confident!

Do whatever you can, to "stay focused".

Once the performance starts you may be surprised how good it feels and how fast the time goes. Don't be yourself, be the character and play the part. Play to the audience but connect with the other characters. Think about eye contact.

I remember going to see a production to review it for a local paper and one of the ladies on stage spent half of the show smiling at, and making eye contact with, a member of her family in the front row. Result – it ruined the production. I say it again – be the character not yourself. Look generally at the audience but not your front row relatives.

When I am in a production and need to look at the audience I will generally aim my eyes at the rear wall of the hall. The one exception to this would be some character in a pantomime – especially the "wicked fairy" who might be aiming to get kids from the audience up on stage.

Don't upstage other actors

In comedies, one of the biggest errors is for actors to begin "upstaging" their colleagues, milking each opportunity for laughter and generally taking centre stage…even when it's rude or inappropriate.

Though the sound of an audience chuckling and clapping can be intoxicating, temper yourself on a regular basis. Be mindful that, unless you're in a one-man (or woman) show, the acting isn't all about you.

If you are doing a pantomime or comedy, there will be lots of times the audience really laughs out loud. Don't deliver your next line until the laughter has died down, because if you do it will be lost in the noise of the laughter.

If you find yourself constantly playing for giggles, ask your director or colleague for assistance and advice. Chances are he or she can give you some pointers on how to stop the mistake of stealing the limelight from your fellow performers.

Okay, so the curtain has come down and the first night is done to great applause from the audience.

So what now – straight out front to greet family and friends.

No, get changed first. It is very unprofessional to go out front while still in costume – always change first and remove make-up, so you go out front as you and not the character you have just played.

KEY POINTS

Do breathing exercises to calm nerves
Concentrate
On stage be the character, Remember the play is not all about you
Be yourself, not your character when greeting family and friends.

Adjudications

So the production week is over, no doubt finishing with a party on the last night.

So how was it for you?

Hopefully a great experience and a very enjoyable social experience. But how good was it really?

One way of getting qualified feedback is to have an adjudicator in on one of the nights. These are people who generally have many years' experience of judging Amdram shows. They may not always have a professional background but are usually members of the Guild of Adjudicators.

For an amateur group, adjudicated drama presents many opportunities, not least of which being able to perform in competitions and at venues with facilities sometimes better than those in their own village hall.

It also gives the opportunity to reach new, larger audiences and to meet other groups and learn and improve from the comments and suggestions of the adjudication itself.

Competitions

Drama festivals and competitions are organised by most regional theatre guilds.

A fairly common occurrence is a one-act play festival. These are usually held annually and the venue changes from group to group, with often this year's winner hosting next year's event.

These can be challenging but fun and generally plays are selected that require little or no set.

Adjudication usually follows with local awards for things like best actor, actress, director, originality and, perhaps, costumes.

One of the benefits of these events is that you get to see other groups and thereby gain ideas about style and presentation, albeit in a one-act play.

So how was it for you? Your production is over, the party has started and everyone is feeling relaxed.

If this was the first time you have appeared on stage you will I hope have found it thrilling and magical. Just think about the audience reaction and applause.

You and your friends have just brought to life some words on a page that were written – possibly in isolation – and completed a triangle. The three sides being , writer, actor and audience.

Whatever the style or genre, a good production will as you have now discovered, create an atmosphere and buzz in the audience.

As I said earlier, live theatre is for all ages with Pantomime – in my opinion – the most important. Why? Because it is usually the first live theatre that many children see. Hopefully it will stimulate their imagination because they will have been able to connect with those on stage, rather than fall asleep in front of a screen.

It is also my belief that live theatre is a very important part of our culture.

It is rewarding and enjoyable, a gift to the local community and above all can be an answer to the stress of work and daily life.

First, at an amateur level it is a very enjoyable hobby, creating a social life with friendships that can last a lifetime.

Secondly it creates a community spirit especially in small villages.

Thirdly, particularly when youngsters are involved in Pantomimes or similar shows it will help build their self confidence and help them understand the importance of team work.

This day and age it seems that football dominates elements of the media but it is a fact that there are more tickets sold annually for live theatre than for football matches.

So now over to you. Get your group started or expand your range and styles of productions and bring the house down.

House lights up

Once again the hall is still
The stage is bare – gone the thrill
Of soft spoke lines and laughter shrill
Costumes, grease paint now are nil.

The lighting box is packed away
As talk begins of future plays.
Director's choice it has to be
But only if they all agree.

Thriller, farce or comedy
Well prepared the cast must be
So sally forth to give a speech
In character, style that you can reach

While funny face, large painted lines
Are just the thing for Pantomime
A story line that stages crime
Is just what makes some actors shine.

Organisations

There are many regional and national drama organisations, societies and guilds which are easy to find on the internet and a good source of support, publicity and information. The following is just a random selection from the many organisations available.

Amdram.net – The Social Network for Amateur Theatre
The Social Network for Amateur Theatre is the only social network dedicated to Amateur Theatre so, as you would expect, the site is full of information.

Association of Irish Musical Societies (AIMS)
An organisation serving and representing amateur music theatre groups in Ireland and Northern Ireland.

Cheshire Theatre Guild
Organises courses and seminars on all aspects of theatre, as well as festivals. Each affiliated society has its own page.

Cumbria Drama Festival
A preliminary round of the All-England Theatre Festival for one-act plays.

Little Theatre Guild
The Little Theatre Guild, now known as the LTG, has been in existence since 1946 to represent the views of amateur theatres across the UK. Membership extends throughout the UK, plus some overseas locations. In particular, membership of the LTG is open only to those amateur theatres that own or lease the theatre premises upon which productions are mounted.

<u>NODA (National Operatic and Dramatic Association)</u>

Has a membership of around 2500 amateur theatre groups and 3000 individual enthusiasts throughout the UK, staging musicals, operas, plays, concerts and pantomimes in a wide variety of performing venues, ranging from the country's leading professional theatres to tiny village halls.

Founded in 1899, NODA is divided into eleven regions, each headed by a regional councillor who sits on the national council (the ruling body of the Association), supported by a network of regional representatives. These 190 volunteers are the vital link to the grass roots of the Association, the amateur theatre groups themselves.

NODA aims:
To give a shared voice to the amateur theatre sector

To help amateur societies and individuals achieve the highest standards of best practice and performance

To provide leadership and advice to enable amateur theatre to tackle the challenges and opportunities of the 21st century

Benefits of membership include access to NODA's advice service at national and regional level, representation to government, funding agencies, the media, and access to conferences, workshops and seminars to help share information on best practice.

NODA also holds an annual residential summer school (with bursaries available), offering training from professional tutors in drama performance, music directing, musical theatre, stage management and other courses for performers, directors and technicians.

Both national and regional news about NODA and its member societies is published as a part of Amateur Stage Magazine. NODA also holds annual national and regional programme and poster competitions, to encourage the highest standards in design.

NODA has an extensive library of theatre books and musical scores.

NODA Scotland
A site giving details of the Scottish Branch of the National Operatic and Dramatic Association.

Nottingham and Notts Amateur Dramatic Association
An association for amateur companies in the Nottinghamshire area. It exists "to promote all aspects of theatre arts, to foster progressive standards and to provide a basis for mutual assistance."

The Scottish Community Drama Association
The SCDA offers a wide range of services. There's news, details of festivals, the organisation, their advisory service, play-writing competitions and workshops, a library of plays, a what's-on section, their youth network, and a net directory.